Colonial America

Work in Colonial America

By Mark Thomas

Children's Press®
A Division of Scholastic Inc.
New York / Toronto / London / Auckland / Sydney
Mexico City / New Delhi / Hong Kong
Danbury, Connecticut

D1210695

Photo Credits: Cover © Catherine Karnow/Corbis; p. 5 © Ted Spiegel/Corbis; p. 7 © Paul A. Souders/Corbis; p. 9 © Dave G. Houser/Corbis; pp. 11, 15 © Colonial Williamsburg Foundation; p. 13 © Wolfgang Kaehler/Corbis; p. 17 © Richard T. Nowitz/Corbis; p. 19 © Annie Griffiths Belt/Corbis

Contributing Editor: Jennifer Silate
Book Design: Erica Clendening

Library of Congress Cataloging-in-Publication Data

Thomas, Mark, 1963–
    Work in Colonial America / by Mark Thomas.
        p. cm. — (Colonial America)
    Includes bibliographical references and index.
    Summary: A simple introduction to various jobs in Colonial America, including those performed by blacksmiths, coopers, and shoemakers.
    ISBN 0-516-23934-1 (lib. bdg.) — ISBN 0-516-23495-1 (pbk.)
    1. United States—Social life and customs—To 1775—Juvenile literature. 2. Working class—United States—History—17th century—Juvenile literature. 3. Working class—United States—History—18th century—Juvenile literature. 4. Work—History—17th century—Juvenile literature. 5. Work—History—18th century—Juvenile literature. [1. Work—History—17th century. 2. Work—History—18th century. 3. United States—Social life and customs—To 1775.] I. Title. II. Colonial America (Children's Press)

E162 .T48 2002
306.3'6'0973—dc21

2001042356

Contents

People in **Colonial America** had many different jobs.

5

Some people who lived in Colonial America were **blacksmiths**.

Blacksmiths made tools from iron.

7

Some people were **coopers**.

They made things from wood.

Coopers made **buckets**, **barrels**, and other things that people needed.

9

Carpenters also made things out of wood.

They built houses and shops.

11

Some people were **cobblers**.

Cobblers made shoes
from leather.

13

In Colonial America, many men and women wore **wigs**.

15

Wigmakers made wigs for people to wear.

17

Many men in Colonial America were farmers.

They grew food for their families.

They also sold food to other people.

19

People in Colonial America worked very hard.

20

21

New Words

barrels (**bar**-uhlz) tall, wooden containers with sides that curve out

blacksmiths (**blak**-smihths) people who make things out of iron

buckets (**buhk**-ihts) pails for carrying things

carpenters (**kar**-puhn-tuhrz) people who build things with wood, like houses and shops

cobblers (**kahb**-luhrz) people who make shoes

Colonial America (kuh-**loh**-nee-uhl uh-**mer**-uh-kuh) the time before the United States became a country (1620–1780)

coopers (**koop**-uhrz) people who make things out of wood, like barrels and buckets

wigmakers (**wihg**-may-kuhrz) people who make wigs

wigs (**wihgz**) head coverings made of hair

To Find Out More

Books

Colonial Times from A to Z
by Bobbie Kalman
Crabtree Publishing

The New Americans: Colonial Times, 1620–1689
by Betsy Maestro
Lothrop, Lee & Shepard Books

Web Site
Colonial Kids: When I Grow Up
http://library.thinkquest.org/J002611F/town.htm
Learn about the different jobs that people in Colonial America had.

Index

About the Author

Mark Thomas has written more than fifty children's and young adult books. He writes and teaches in Florida.

Reading Consultants

Kris Flynn, Coordinator, Small School District Literacy, The San Diego County Office of Education

Shelly Forys, Certified Reading Recovery Specialist, W.J. Zahnow Elementary School, Waterloo, IL

Sue McAdams, Former President of the North Texas Reading Council of the IRA, and Early Literacy Consultant, Dallas, TX